CW00516079

- Copyright © 2020 -

All rights reserved. No part of this publication may be reproduced, distributed or transmitted in any form or by any means (electronic, mechanical, photocopying, recording or otherwise) without the prior written permission of the author.

KNITTING Projects Tracking For Child

This Journal belongs to

_____

INDEX

N°	Project Name	Page
1		8
2		10
3		12
4		14
5		16
6		18
7		20
8		22
9		24
10		26
11		28
12		30
13		32
14		34
15		36
16		38
17		40
18		42
19		44
20		46

PROJECT 1

Made for _____   Size _____

Occasion _____   Dimensions _____

Start Date _____   Total Fee _____

End Date _____   Difficulty

Material (wool-yarn / needles / buttons / ... etc)

Sketch

8

Technique

Instructions

Customization ideas

Finish Project Photo

Wool / Yarn
Sample & Label

Notes

What I Learned

What I need to improve

What I liked

PROJECT 2

Realization

Made for _____   Size _____

Occasion _____   Dimensions _____

Start Date _____   Total Fee _____

End Date _____   Difficulty

Material (wool-yarn / needles / buttons / ... etc)

Sketch

10

Technique

Instructions

Customization ideas

Finish Project Photo

Wool / Yarn
Sample & Label

Notes

What I Learned

What I need to improve

What I liked

PROJECT 3

Made for _____ Size _____

Occasion _____ Dimensions _____

Start Date _____ Total Fee _____

End Date _____ Difficulty

Material (wool-yarn / needles / buttons / ... etc)

Sketch

Technique

Instructions

Customization ideas

Finish Project Photo

Wool / Yarn
Sample & Label

Notes

What I Learned

What I need to improve

What I liked

PROJECT 4

Realization

Made for _____   Size _____

Occasion _____   Dimensions _____

Start Date _____   Total Fee _____

End Date _____   Difficulty

Material (wool-yarn / needles / buttons / ... etc)

Sketch

14

Technique

Instructions

Customization ideas

Finish Project Photo

Wool / Yarn
Sample & Label

Notes

What I Learned

What I need to improve

What I liked

PROJECT 5

Realization

Made for _____ Size _____

Occasion _____ Dimensions _____

Start Date _____ Total Fee _____

End Date _____ Difficulty

Material (wool-yarn / needles / buttons / ... etc)

Sketch

16

Technique

Instructions

Customization ideas

Finish Project Photo

Wool / Yarn
Sample & Label

Notes

What I Learned

What I need to improve

What I liked

PROJECT 6

Realization

Made for _____   Size _____

Occasion _____   Dimensions _____

Start Date _____   Total Fee _____

End Date _____   Difficulty

Material (wool-yarn / needles / buttons / ... etc)

Sketch

18

Technique

Instructions

Customization ideas

Finish Project Photo

Wool / Yarn
Sample & Label

Notes

What I Learned

What I need to improve

What I liked

PROJECT 7

Realization

Made for _____   Size _____

Occasion _____   Dimensions _____

Start Date _____   Total Fee _____

End Date _____   Difficulty

Material (wool-yarn / needles / buttons / ... etc)

Sketch

Technique

Instructions

Customization ideas

Finish Project Photo

Wool / Yarn
Sample & Label

Notes

What I Learned

What I need to improve

What I liked

PROJECT 8

Made for _____ Size _____

Occasion _____ Dimensions _____

Start Date _____ Total Fee _____

End Date _____ Difficulty 🧶 🧶🧶 🧶🧶🧶

Material (wool-yarn / needles / buttons / ... etc)

Sketch

Technique

Instructions

Customization ideas

Finish Project Photo

Wool / Yarn
Sample & Label

Notes

What I Learned

What I need to improve

What I liked

PROJECT 9

Realization

Made for _____   Size _____

Occasion _____   Dimensions _____

Start Date _____   Total Fee _____

End Date _____   Difficulty

Material (wool-yarn / needles / buttons / ... etc)

Sketch

24

Technique

Instructions

Customization ideas

Finish Project Photo

Wool / Yarn
Sample & Label

Notes

What I Learned

What I need to improve

What I liked

PROJECT 10

Realization

Made for _____   Size _____

Occasion _____   Dimensions _____

Start Date _____   Total Fee _____

End Date _____   Difficulty 🧶 🧶🧶 🧶🧶🧶

Material (wool-yarn / needles / buttons / ... etc)

Sketch

Technique

Instructions

Customization ideas

Finish Project Photo

Wool / Yarn
Sample & Label

Notes

What I Learned

What I need to improve

What I liked

PROJECT 11

Made for _____   Size _____

Occasion _____   Dimensions _____

Start Date _____   Total Fee _____

End Date _____   Difficulty

Material (wool-yarn / needles / buttons / ... etc)

Sketch

28

Technique

Instructions

Customization ideas

Finish Project Photo

Wool / Yarn
Sample & Label

Notes

What I Learned

What I need to improve

What I liked

PROJECT 12

Realization

Made for _____   Size _____

Occasion _____   Dimensions _____

Start Date _____   Total Fee _____

End Date _____   Difficulty 🧶   🧶🧶   🧶🧶🧶

Material (wool-yarn / needles / buttons / ... etc)

Sketch

Technique

Instructions

Customization ideas

Finish Project Photo

Wool / Yarn
Sample & Label

Notes

What I Learned

What I need to improve

What I liked

PROJECT 13

Realization

Made for _____   Size _____

Occasion _____   Dimensions _____

Start Date _____   Total Fee _____

End Date _____   Difficulty 🧶 🧶🧶 🧶🧶🧶

Material (wool-yarn / needles / buttons / ... etc)

Sketch

32

Technique

Instructions

Customization ideas

Finish Project Photo

Wool / Yarn
Sample & Label

Notes

What I Learned

What I need to improve

What I liked

PROJECT 14

Made for _____   Size _____

Occasion _____   Dimensions _____

Start Date _____   Total Fee _____

End Date _____   Difficulty

Material (wool-yarn / needles / buttons / ... etc)

Sketch

34

Technique

Instructions

Customization ideas

Wool / Yarn
Sample & Label

Finish Project Photo

Notes

What I Learned

What I need to improve

What I liked

PROJECT 15

Made for _____ Size _____

Occasion _____ Dimensions _____

Start Date _____ Total Fee _____

End Date _____ Difficulty

Material (wool-yarn / needles / buttons / ... etc)

Sketch

Technique

Instructions

Customization ideas

Finish Project Photo

Wool / Yarn
Sample & Label

Notes

What I Learned

What I need to improve

What I liked

PROJECT 16

Realization

Made for _____   Size _____
Occasion _____   Dimensions _____
Start Date _____   Total Fee _____
End Date _____   Difficulty

Material (wool-yarn / needles / buttons / ... etc)

Sketch

Technique

Instructions

Customization ideas

Wool / Yarn
Sample & Label

Finish Project Photo

Notes

What I Learned

What I need to improve

What I liked

PROJECT 17

Made for _____   Size _____

Occasion _____   Dimensions _____

Start Date _____   Total Fee _____

End Date _____   Difficulty 🧶 🧶🧶 🧶🧶🧶

Material (wool-yarn / needles / buttons / ... etc)

Sketch

40

Technique

Instructions

Customization ideas

Finish Project Photo

Wool / Yarn
Sample & Label

Notes

What I Learned

What I need to improve

What I liked

PROJECT 18

Made for _____ Size _____

Occasion _____ Dimensions _____

Start Date _____ Total Fee _____

End Date _____ Difficulty

Material (wool-yarn / needles / buttons / ... etc)

Sketch

Technique

Instructions

Customization ideas

Finish Project Photo

Wool / Yarn
Sample & Label

Notes

What I Learned

What I need to improve

What I liked

PROJECT 19

Made for _____ Size _____

Occasion _____ Dimensions _____

Start Date _____ Total Fee _____

End Date _____ Difficulty 🧶 🧶🧶 🧶🧶🧶

Material (wool-yarn / needles / buttons / ... etc)

Sketch

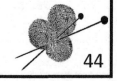

Technique

Instructions

Customization ideas

Wool / Yarn
Sample & Label

Finish Project Photo

Notes

What I Learned

What I need to improve

What I liked

PROJECT 20

Realization

Made for _____ Size _____

Occasion _____ Dimensions _____

Start Date _____ Total Fee _____

End Date _____ Difficulty

Material (wool-yarn / needles / buttons / ... etc)

Sketch

Technique

Instructions

Customization ideas

Finish Project Photo

Wool / Yarn
Sample & Label

Notes

What I Learned

What I need to improve

What I liked

PROJECT 21

Realization

Made for _____   Size _____

Occasion _____   Dimensions _____

Start Date _____   Total Fee _____

End Date _____   Difficulty

Material (wool-yarn / needles / buttons / ... etc)

Sketch

48

Technique

Instructions

Customization ideas

Finish Project Photo

Wool / Yarn
Sample & Label

Notes

What I Learned

What I need to improve

What I liked

PROJECT 22

Realization

Made for _____ Size _____

Occasion _____ Dimensions _____

Start Date _____ Total Fee _____

End Date _____ Difficulty 🧶 🧶🧶 🧶🧶🧶

Material (wool-yarn / needles / buttons / ... etc)

Sketch

50

Technique

Instructions

Customization ideas

Finish Project Photo

Wool / Yarn
Sample & Label

Notes

What I Learned

What I need to improve

What I liked

Realization

Made for _____   Size _____

Occasion _____   Dimensions _____

Start Date _____   Total Fee _____

End Date _____   Difficulty

Material (wool-yarn / needles / buttons / ... etc)

Sketch

Technique

Instructions

Customization ideas

Wool / Yarn
Sample & Label

Finish Project Photo

Notes

What I Learned

What I need to improve

What I liked

PROJECT 24

Made for _____ Size _____

Occasion _____ Dimensions _____

Start Date _____ Total Fee _____

End Date _____ Difficulty

Material (wool-yarn / needles / buttons / ... etc)

Sketch

Technique

Instructions

Customization ideas

Finish Project Photo

Wool / Yarn
Sample & Label

Notes

What I Learned

What I need to improve

What I liked

PROJECT 25

Made for _____   Size _____

Occasion _____   Dimensions _____

Start Date _____   Total Fee _____

End Date _____   Difficulty 🧶   🧶🧶   🧶🧶🧶

Material (wool-yarn / needles / buttons / ... etc)

Sketch

56

Technique

Instructions

Customization ideas

Finish Project Photo

Wool / Yarn
Sample & Label

Notes

What I Learned

What I need to improve

What I liked

PROJECT 26

Realization

Made for _____

Occasion _____

Start Date _____

End Date _____

Size _____

Dimensions _____

Total Fee _____

Difficulty

Material (wool-yarn / needles / buttons / ... etc)

Sketch

Technique

Instructions

Customization ideas

Finish Project Photo

Wool / Yarn
Sample & Label

Notes

What I Learned

What I need to improve

What I liked

PROJECT 27

Made for _____ Size _____

Occasion _____ Dimensions _____

Start Date _____ Total Fee _____

End Date _____ Difficulty

Material (wool-yarn / needles / buttons / ... etc)

Sketch

Technique

Instructions

Customization ideas

Finish Project Photo

Wool / Yarn
Sample & Label

Notes

What I Learned

What I need to improve

What I liked

PROJECT 28

Made for _____   Size _____

Occasion _____   Dimensions _____

Start Date _____   Total Fee _____

End Date _____   Difficulty

Material (wool-yarn / needles / buttons / ... etc)

Sketch

62

Technique

Instructions

Customization ideas

Finish Project Photo

Wool / Yarn
Sample & Label

Notes

What I Learned

What I need to improve

What I liked

PROJECT 29

Realization

Made for _____   Size _____

Occasion _____   Dimensions _____

Start Date _____   Total Fee _____

End Date _____   Difficulty

Material (wool-yarn / needles / buttons / ... etc)

Sketch

Technique

Instructions

Customization ideas

Finish Project Photo

Wool / Yarn
Sample & Label

Notes

What I Learned

What I need to improve

What I liked

PROJECT 30

Realization

Made for _____   Size _____

Occasion _____   Dimensions _____

Start Date _____   Total Fee _____

End Date _____   Difficulty

Material (wool-yarn / needles / buttons / ... etc)

Sketch

66

Technique

Instructions

Customization ideas

Finish Project Photo

Wool / Yarn
Sample & Label

Notes

What I Learned

What I need to improve

What I liked

PROJECT 31

Realization

Made for _____   Size _____

Occasion _____   Dimensions _____

Start Date _____   Total Fee _____

End Date _____   Difficulty 🧶 🧶🧶 🧶🧶🧶

Material (wool-yarn / needles / buttons / ... etc)

Sketch

Technique

Instructions

Customization ideas

Finish Project Photo

Wool / Yarn
Sample & Label

Notes

What I Learned

What I need to improve

What I liked

PROJECT 32

Realization

Made for _____   Size _____

Occasion _____   Dimensions _____

Start Date _____   Total Fee _____

End Date _____   Difficulty

Material (wool-yarn / needles / buttons / ... etc)

Sketch

Technique

Instructions

Customization ideas

Wool / Yarn
Sample & Label

Finish Project Photo

Notes

What I Learned

What I need to improve

What I liked

PROJECT 33

Realization

Made for _____   Size _____

Occasion _____   Dimensions _____

Start Date _____   Total Fee _____

End Date _____   Difficulty

Material (wool-yarn / needles / buttons / ... etc)

Sketch

Technique

Instructions

Customization ideas

Finish Project Photo

Wool / Yarn
Sample & Label

Notes

What I Learned

What I need to improve

What I liked

PROJECT 34

Realization

Made for _____ Size _____

Occasion _____ Dimensions _____

Start Date _____ Total Fee _____

End Date _____ Difficulty

Material (wool-yarn / needles / buttons / ... etc)

Sketch

Technique

Instructions

Customization ideas

Finish Project Photo

Wool / Yarn
Sample & Label

Notes

What I Learned

What I need to improve

What I liked

PROJECT 35

Made for _____ Size _____

Occasion _____ Dimensions _____

Start Date _____ Total Fee _____

End Date _____ Difficulty

Material (wool-yarn / needles / buttons / ... etc)

Sketch

76

Technique

Instructions

Customization ideas

Finish Project Photo

Wool / Yarn
Sample & Label

Notes

What I Learned

What I need to improve

What I liked

PROJECT 36

Realization

Made for _____   Size _____

Occasion _____   Dimensions _____

Start Date _____   Total Fee _____

End Date _____   Difficulty 🧶 🧶🧶 🧶🧶🧶

Material (wool-yarn / needles / buttons / ... etc)

Sketch

78

Technique

Instructions

Customization ideas

Finish Project Photo

Wool / Yarn
Sample & Label

Notes

What I Learned

What I need to improve

What I liked

PROJECT 37

Made for _____   Size _____

Occasion _____   Dimensions _____

Start Date _____   Total Fee _____

End Date _____   Difficulty

Material (wool-yarn / needles / buttons / ... etc)

Sketch

Technique

Instructions

Customization ideas

Finish Project Photo

Wool / Yarn
Sample & Label

Notes

What I Learned

What I need to improve

What I liked

PROJECT 38

Realization

Made for _____   Size _____

Occasion _____   Dimensions _____

Start Date _____   Total Fee _____

End Date _____   Difficulty   🧶   🧶🧶   🧶🧶🧶

Material (wool-yarn / needles / buttons / ... etc)

Sketch

82

Technique

Instructions

Customization ideas

Finish Project Photo

Wool / Yarn
Sample & Label

Notes

What I Learned

What I need to improve

What I liked

PROJECT 39

Realization

Made for _____   Size _____

Occasion _____   Dimensions _____

Start Date _____   Total Fee _____

End Date _____   Difficulty

Material (wool-yarn / needles / buttons / ... etc)

Sketch

84

Technique

Instructions

Customization ideas

Finish Project Photo

Wool / Yarn
Sample & Label

Notes

What I Learned

What I need to improve

What I liked

PROJECT 40

Realization

Made for _____   Size _____

Occasion _____   Dimensions _____

Start Date _____   Total Fee _____

End Date _____   Difficulty 🧶 🧶🧶 🧶🧶🧶

Material (wool-yarn / needles / buttons / ... etc)

Sketch

86

Technique

Instructions

Customization ideas

Finish Project Photo

Wool / Yarn
Sample & Label

Notes

What I Learned

What I need to improve

What I liked

PROJECT 41

Made for _____

Occasion _____

Start Date _____

End Date _____

Size _____

Dimensions _____

Total Fee _____

Difficulty 🧶 🧶🧶 🧶🧶🧶

Material (wool-yarn / needles / buttons / ... etc)

Sketch

88

Technique

Instructions

Customization ideas

Wool / Yarn
Sample & Label

Finish Project Photo

Notes

What I Learned

What I need to improve

What I liked

PROJECT 42

Realization

Made for _____ Size _____

Occasion _____ Dimensions _____

Start Date _____ Total Fee _____

End Date _____ Difficulty 🧶 🧶🧶 🧶🧶🧶

Material (wool-yarn / needles / buttons / ... etc)

Sketch

Technique

Instructions

Customization ideas

Finish Project Photo

Wool / Yarn
Sample & Label

Notes

What I Learned

What I need to improve

What I liked

PROJECT 43

Realization

Made for _____ Size _____

Occasion _____ Dimensions _____

Start Date _____ Total Fee _____

End Date _____ Difficulty 🧶 🧶🧶 🧶🧶🧶

Material (wool-yarn / needles / buttons / ... etc)

Sketch

92

Technique

Instructions

Customization ideas

Finish Project Photo

Wool / Yarn
Sample & Label

Notes

What I Learned

What I need to improve

What I liked

PROJECT 44

Realization

Made for _____ Size _____

Occasion _____ Dimensions _____

Start Date _____ Total Fee _____

End Date _____ Difficulty 🧶 🧶🧶 🧶🧶🧶

Material (wool-yarn / needles / buttons / ... etc)

Sketch

Technique

Instructions

Customization ideas

Finish Project Photo

Wool / Yarn
Sample & Label

Notes

What I Learned

What I need to improve

What I liked

PROJECT 45

Realization

Made for _____ Size _____

Occasion _____ Dimensions _____

Start Date _____ Total Fee _____

End Date _____ Difficulty

Material (wool-yarn / needles / buttons / ... etc)

Sketch

Technique

Instructions

Customization ideas

Wool / Yarn
Sample & Label

Finish Project Photo

Notes

What I Learned

What I need to improve

What I liked

PROJECT 46

Realization

Made for _____ Size _____

Occasion _____ Dimensions _____

Start Date _____ Total Fee _____

End Date _____ Difficulty 🧶 🧶🧶 🧶🧶🧶

Material (wool-yarn / needles / buttons / ... etc)

Sketch

Technique

Instructions

Customization ideas

Finish Project Photo

Wool / Yarn
Sample & Label

Notes

What I Learned

What I need to improve

What I liked

PROJECT 47

Realization

Made for _____ Size _____

Occasion _____ Dimensions _____

Start Date _____ Total Fee _____

End Date _____ Difficulty

Material (wool-yarn / needles / buttons / ... etc)

Sketch

100

Technique

Instructions

Customization ideas

Finish Project Photo

Wool / Yarn
Sample & Label

Notes

What I Learned

What I need to improve

What I liked

PROJECT 48

Realization

Made for _____ Size _____

Occasion _____ Dimensions _____

Start Date _____ Total Fee _____

End Date _____ Difficulty 🧶 🧶🧶 🧶🧶🧶

Material (wool-yarn / needles / buttons / ... etc)

Sketch

102

Technique

Instructions

Customization ideas

Finish Project Photo

Wool / Yarn
Sample & Label

Notes

What I Learned

What I need to improve

What I liked

PROJECT 49

Realization

Made for _____ Size _____

Occasion _____ Dimensions _____

Start Date _____ Total Fee _____

End Date _____ Difficulty 🧶 🧶🧶 🧶🧶🧶

Material (wool-yarn / needles / buttons / ... etc)

Sketch

104

Technique

Instructions

Customization ideas

Finish Project Photo

Wool / Yarn
Sample & Label

Notes

What I Learned

What I need to improve

What I liked

PROJECT 50

Realization

Made for _____   Size _____

Occasion _____   Dimensions _____

Start Date _____   Total Fee _____

End Date _____   Difficulty

Material (wool-yarn / needles / buttons / ... etc)

Sketch

106

Technique

Instructions

Customization ideas

Finish Project Photo

Wool / Yarn
Sample & Label

Notes

What I Learned

What I need to improve

What I liked

Printed in Great Britain
by Amazon

38072025R00059